This Book Is The Property of
CALEDONIA COMMUNITY SCHOOLS
BOOK NO. 7853
DATE OF PUB. _____
SUBJECT _____
DATE _____
User agrees to pay for any
damage and excessive wear
caused by normal usage.

YEAR	STUDENT	CONDITION

Exploring Science ORANGE BOOK

MILO K. BLECHA
Professor of
Science Education
College of Education
University of Arizona

PETER C. GEGA
Elementary-School
Science Specialist
San Diego State University
San Diego, California

MURIEL GREEN
Supervisor of Science
Board of Education
New York City, Dist. 29
Queens Village, New York

Reviewer/Consultants

Ms. Ruth M. Buck
Teacher, A. Burnet Rhett
Elementary School
Charleston, South Carolina

Lorraine B. Ide
Elementary Science Supervisor
Springfield Public Schools
Springfield, Massachusetts

Imogene C. Moody
Master Teacher/Counselor
Raymond Elementary School
Chicago, Illinois

Cynthia McC. Smith
Teacher, Mitchell
Elementary School
Charleston, South Carolina

Neva Lowe Weaver
Elementary Teacher
Norman Public Schools
Norman, Oklahoma

LAIDLAW BROTHERS • PUBLISHERS

A Division of Doubleday & Company, Inc.

RIVER FOREST, ILLINOIS

Irvine, California   Chamblee, Georgia   Dallas, Texas   Toronto, Canada

The Laidlaw Exploring Science Program

Exploring Science ORANGE   Exploring Science BROWN

Exploring Science GOLD   Exploring Science GREEN

Exploring Science BLUE   Exploring Science RED

Exploring Matter and Energy

Exploring Living Things

Exploring Earth and Space

Project Director   Thomas E. Navta / *Production Director*   LaVergne G. Niequist / *Art Director*   Gloria J. Muczynski / *Photo Researcher*   William A. Cassin / *Staff Editors*   Helen Fitzpatrick, Patricia L. Snyder / *Production Supervisors*   Donna E. Delaine, Marilyn Scheda / *Production Associate*   Dee Staahl / *Artists*   Patty Boyd, Paul Hazelrigg, Donald Meighan, Larry Mikec / *Cover Design*   Donald Meighan

Acknowledgments

The publishers wish to express their appreciation to the following sources for their permission to reproduce the photographs on the pages indicated. alfa studio: 9, 14, 15, 16 (left), 17, 19, 21 (both), 59. Arejay, 117 (top). Artstreet: 50 (top and bottom right), 56 (right), 74 (bottom right), 112 (bottom right), 130 (top right), 131 (top). *Robert Borja;* Courtesy of the Faulkner School, Chicago: 126, 132, 133, 136, 137. *Robert Davis,* 123 (right). *Dr. E. R. Degginger:* 8 (right), 22, 26 (top left and bottom right), 30 (left), 44 (top right), 51 (top left), 52 (both), 55 (top), 80 (left). *Dr. E. R. Degginger/Wm. D. Griffin,* 42 (top). *Phil Degginger:* 28 (right), 29 (right), 32 (bottom), 34 (both), 46. A. Devaney, Inc., 60 (right). De Wys, Inc., 83 (bottom right).

(Acknowledgments continued on page 144)

Copyright © 1976 by **Laidlaw Brothers, Publishers** A DIVISION OF DOUBLEDAY & COMPANY, INC.

All rights reserved. No part of this publication may be reproduced or transmitted in any form or by any means, electronic or mechanical, including photocopy, recording, or any information storage or retrieval system, without permission in writing from the publisher.

ISBN 0-8445-5521-5   PRINTED IN THE UNITED STATES OF AMERICA

456789 10 11 12 13 14 15   4321098

CONTENTS

3

1 Your Senses

How is Mark finding out about things around him?

How do you find out about things around you?

Seeing

How are these children finding out about things?

How does seeing help you find out about things?

FINDING OUT

▶ Make a magnifying glass
like the one in the picture.

▶ Hold some small things
under it.

Does your magnifying glass help you
find out about things? If so, how?

Hearing

What sounds are being made
in the pictures?

How does hearing help you
find out about things?

Touching

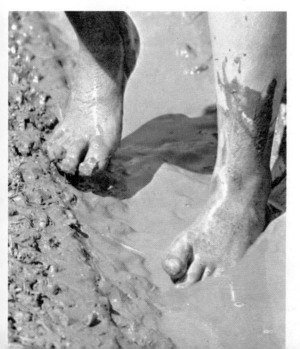

What are these children
finding out by touching?
How is touching important
to you?

13

FINDING OUT

- ► Close your eyes.
- ► Hold a glass of warm water and a glass of cold water.
- ► Tell which glass of water feels warm and which feels cold.

► Taste some foods.
► Tell which food feels hard
and which feels soft.

How else might things feel to you?
What other parts of your body
can you feel with?

Smelling

How are these children
finding out about things?

► Close your eyes.
► Have a friend hold some
  things in front of your nose.
► Guess what each thing is.

   Which things did you
guess right?
   Is smelling important to you?
If so, why?

Tasting

What are some foods
you like the taste of?

► Taste some foods.
► Tell which foods taste sweet.
► Tell how the other foods taste.

Is tasting important to you?
If so, why?

Smelling and tasting

Does smelling help you taste foods?
How might you find out?

FINDING OUT

- ► Close your eyes.
- ► Hold your nose shut.
- ► Try guessing what some foods are by tasting them.

Might smelling the foods help you taste them? Try finding out.

Words to Know

seeing   touching   tasting

hearing   smelling

Picture to Think About

How are these children finding out about things around them?

Questions to Answer

1. How does seeing help you find out about things?
2. How does hearing help you find out about things?
3. How does touching help you find out about things?
4. How does smelling help you find out about things?
5. How does tasting help you find out about foods?

Fun Things to Do

Draw some pictures.
Show some ways seeing
and hearing help you.
Show some ways touching, smelling,
and tasting help you.

Have a tasting party.
Taste some foods you
have never tasted before.

2 Living Things

When did Kevin know
his brush was living?

What are some other
living things?

Kinds of living things

Which of these living things are plants?

Which of these living things are animals?

How are you different from other living things?

FINDING OUT

► Find some things outside.
► Find things that are not living.
► Find things that are living.

28

Which of your things are not living?
Which of your living things are plants?
Which are animals?

Moving

Which things can move by themselves?

How did the plant move?
What do you think made
the plant move?

Growing and changing

Which things in the pictures can grow?

Which things cannot grow? Why?
How do some living things change
as they grow?

FINDING OUT

► Plant many kinds of seeds.
► Take care of your plants.
► Watch them grow.

Which plants grew the most?
How did the plants change?

FINDING OUT

▶ Bring in pictures of you when you were little.
▶ Guess which picture belongs to each of your friends.

How did your friends grow and change?

How much did you grow? How can you tell?

New living things

Many new plants come from seeds.
Where do seeds come from?

Baby animals come from their
mother and father.

Where have you seen a baby
with its mother and father?

KETTLE LAKE SCHOOL

37

Care of new living things

How do some living things
care for their babies?

Needs of plants

What things do plants need?

FINDING OUT

▶ Get 3 plants.
▶ Put labels on the plants.
▶ Do as the labels say.

No Water

Water and Light

Water and No Light

Which plant grew best? Why?

Needs of animals

What things do animals need?

FINDING OUT

► Find some animals to raise.
► Give them what they need.

What things do your animals need?

Your needs

44

What things do children need?
How do you get the things you need?

Words to Know

living things   plants   mother
need   animals   father
care   baby   change
grow

Picture to Think About

What things do these
living things need?

Questions to Answer

1. What are some things
   living things can do?
2. What do plants need to live?
3. What do animals need to live?
4. What are some things you need?

Fun Things to Do

Visit a zoo or a pet store.
Find out about the animals.
Find out what they need.

Make a scrapbook.
Put pictures of living things
in your scrapbook.
Show what the living things need.

3 Sorting

How did Maria sort things?

What things did Happy sort?

What things have you sorted?

How things are alike

What things in the pictures are alike?

How are they alike?

How things are different

What things in the pictures are different?

How are they different?

Sorting by color

What colors do you see
in the picture?

How have these things
been sorted?

FINDING OUT

► Find some things
of different colors.
► Sort them by their color.

What things around you
are sorted by color?

Sorting by size

Which thing in each picture is big?

Which thing in each picture is little?

How might you sort these things?

Sorting by shape

Find the different shapes
in these pictures.

Find the different shapes
in your room.

FINDING OUT

► Go outside.
► Find something ◯ .
► Find something ☐ .
► Find something △ .

What other shapes
can you find outside?

➤ Cut out shapes from
   colored paper.
➤ Put the cutouts in a pile.
➤ Sort them by shape.

How else can you sort
the cutouts? Try it.

59

Sorting by feeling

Which things do you think
feel smooth?
Which things feel rough?

There are other ways to sort
things by feeling them.
How might you sort these things?

FINDING OUT

- ► Bring in some small things.
- ► Tell which things feel rough.
- ► Tell which things feel smooth.

How might you sort these things?

➤ Find some things that are hard.
➤ Find some things that are soft.
➤ Close your eyes.
➤ Sort the things you found.

How did you sort your things?

63

Sorting by two differences

Find something big and ○ .
Find something long and green.

Find something hard and ☐.
Find something little and yellow.
Sort these things in other ways.
Use two differences.

Sorting for selling

How have these things been sorted for selling?

FINDING OUT

▶ Bring in some little toys.
▶ Make a toy store.
▶ Sort the toys.

How did you sort the toys?

Sorting at home

How are these people sorting their food?

What things do you sort at home?

FINDING OUT

▶ Put everyone's shoes in a pile.
▶ Try to find your shoes.

▶ Sort the shoes in some way.
▶ Try to find your shoes now.

How does sorting help you find things?

Words to Know

alike   color   soft
different   shape   rough
differences   feel   smooth
sort   hard

Picture to Think About

How is this child
sorting things?
How is sorting helpful?

70

Questions to Answer

1. What are some different ways to sort things?
2. When have you had to sort things?
3. How has sorting helped you?

Fun Things to Do

Collect some buttons or other things.
Sort them in many ways.

Cut out some pictures of things
to eat and drink.
Make a grocery store.
Sort the things to sell.

4 Light and Shadows

Why did the bug look big?

When do you make a shadow?

Light

74

Where is the light coming from?
What other things give you light?

Shadows

Find the shadows.
How do you think
shadows are made?

▶ Cut some things out of paper.
▶ Put each thing in front of a light.

What happened when you stopped some of the light?

Can you make a shadow in the dark? Try it.

► Have your friends
make shadows.

How can you tell what
is making each shadow?

- Put something close to a light.
- Look at its shadow.
- Now move it away from the light.

How did the shadow change?

Moving shadows

What things can your shadow do? Why?

FINDING OUT

▶ Try to step on someone's shadow.

What games can you play with shadows?

Finding the light

Which way is the light coming from?

How can you tell where the light
is coming from?

➤ Show where the missing shadow
should be.

How did you know where
the shadow should be?

84

FINDING OUT

► Walk under a light.
► Watch your shadow.

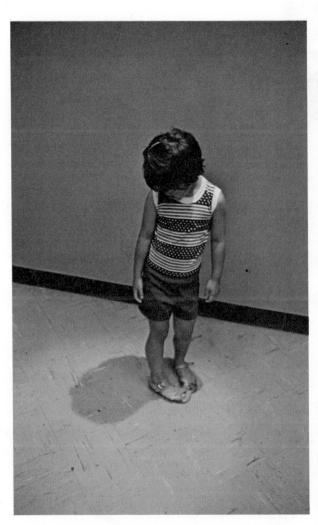

How did your shadow move?
Why did your shadow move?

Shadows in the morning

The sun is in the east in the early morning.

How can shadows help the girls find the east?

FINDING OUT

- ► Go outside early in the morning.
- ► Face the east.
- ► Face the other way.
- ► Find your shadow each time.

Where is your shadow when you
face the east in the morning?

87

Shadows in the afternoon

The sun is in the west in the late afternoon.

How can shadows help these people find the west?

► Go outside in the late afternoon.
► Face the west.
► Have a friend face the east.

Which way do shadows point in the afternoon?

89

Shadows at noon

Why are shadows small at noon?

FINDING OUT

▶ Make a shadow outside
or by a window.
▶ Mark the shadow every hour.

What made the shadow move?
How is the sun like a clock?

Changing shadows

What happened to the shadows?

FINDING OUT

- ▶ Draw a shadow in the early morning.
- ▶ Draw the shadow of the same thing at noon.
- ▶ Draw the shadow in the afternoon.

How did the shadows change?

93

Words to Know

light   morning   east

shadows   noon   west

sun   afternoon

Picture to Think About

What time of day
is it in the picture?
How can you tell?

94

Questions to Answer

1. What things give you light?
2. How can you make a shadow?
3. How can your shadow help you find the east and the west?
4. How can your shadow help you tell time?

Fun Things to Do

Draw a picture from a shadow.
Color it just one color.

Make funny shadows on the wall.
Have a shadow show.

Why did Cindy want time
to go by fast?

When have you wanted time
to go by fast?

A day

From morning to morning is one whole day.

From afternoon to afternoon is one whole day.

What other times can be used to mark one whole day?

Daytime and nighttime

Daytime and nighttime
are parts of a day.
What things do you do
at each of these times?

100

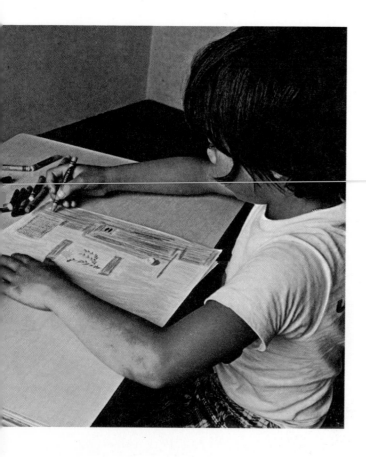

► Draw pictures of things you do every day.

► Put your pictures in order of time.

When do you do these things every day?

Telling the time of day

Clocks tell you when it is time for school.

Clocks tell you when it is time for lunch.

When else do clocks help you?

FINDING OUT

➤ Get a can.
➤ Make a small hole in the can.
➤ Fill the can with water.
➤ Count until the water runs out.

How can a water clock show you that some time has gone by?

Minutes

Minutes help tell time.
When do minutes seem
to go by slowly?

When do minutes seem
to go by fast?

- ► Find a minute timer.
- ► Turn it upside down.
- ► Close your eyes until you think a minute has passed.

How close was your guess?

Yesterday, today, and tomorrow

yesterday

today

Yesterday we rode our bikes.
Today we are playing ball.
What did you do yesterday?

106

Tomorrow we will play
with the trains.
    What will you do tomorrow?

107

A week

Sunday

Thursday

Monday

Friday

Tuesday

Wednesday

Saturday

From Sunday through Saturday is a week.

What are some things you do on each day of the week?

A month

How many days does
the month in the picture have?

In what month
is your birthday?

FINDING OUT

▶ Make a calendar for this month.
▶ Draw a cake on each day that is someone's birthday.
▶ Draw something for some of the other days.

How can a calendar help you?

A year

What are some things that
happen once a year?

The seasons

The seasons change during a year.
What is it like in fall?
What is it like in winter?

114

What is it like in spring?
What is it like in summer?

FINDING OUT

- Have your class make pictures of the four seasons.
- Work on the season you like best.
- Put the pictures in order.
- Start with fall.

How are the seasons different?

Words to Know

day	minute	week
nighttime	yesterday	month
clock	today	year
time	tomorrow	seasons

Picture to Think About

About what time of day is it?
What will the children do now?
When will they come back to school?

Questions to Answer

1. What are some times that can mark one whole day?
2. What things do you do once a week?
3. What things happen just once a year?
4. What are the seasons of the year?

Fun Things to Do

Have your friends hide something.
Ask them to sing a song.
Find it in the time they take
to sing the song.

Find some things besides clocks and
calendars that help people tell time.

6 Spaces and Places

Why did Charlene skate into the mud?

When is it helpful to know what is
in front of you or in back of you?

Front and back

What things are
in front of the girls?
What things are
in back of the girls?

These children know what is in front and what is in back of them. Why might this be important?

FINDING OUT

- ► Name some things you see in front of you.
- ► Name some things in back of you.
- ► Turn around.

Now which things are in front of you? In back of you? Why?

FINDING OUT

- ► Draw a horse and a cowboy.
- ► Cut out the cowboy.
- ► Put the horse on a wall.
- ► Close your eyes.
- ► Try to put the cowboy on the horse in front of you.

How close did you come?

Left and right

What things are on the girl's left?

What things are on your left?

What things are on
the boy's right?

What things are on
your right?

► Stand up.
► Hop on your left foot.

► Shake your right arm.
► Close your left eye.

► Cover your right foot with your left hand.
► Cover your left eye with your right hand.
► Hold your right knee with your right hand.

Which of these things could you do?

What games can you make up using the words *right* and *left*?

Higher and lower

What things are higher than the children's head?

What things are lower than
the children's head?

FINDING OUT

➤ Blow up a balloon.
➤ Move around while keeping the balloon higher than your head.

How did you keep the balloon higher than your head?

► Move around while keeping the balloon lower than your head.

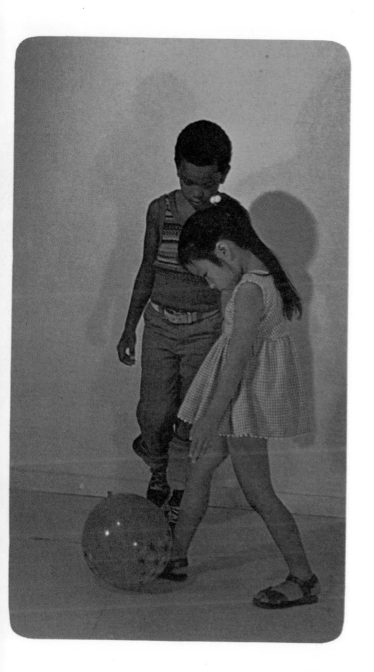

How did you keep the balloon lower than your head?

Near and far

What things are near the girls?

What things are
far from the boys?

► Pick something in the room
   while everybody's eyes are closed.
► Do not tell anyone
   what you picked.
► Walk around the room.

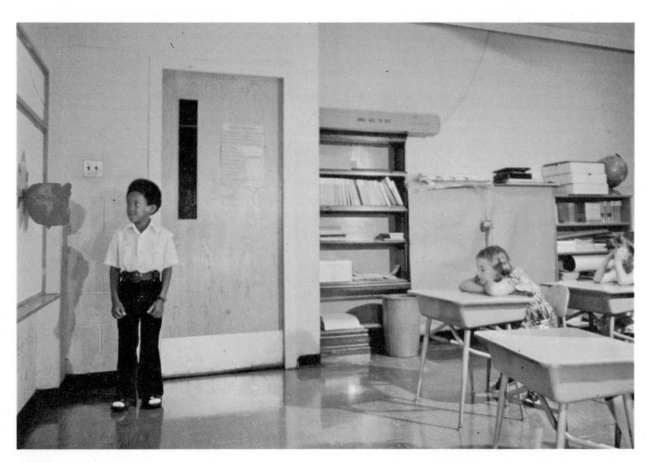

► Have everyone guess when you are
  near to or far from what you picked.

► Have everyone try to guess
  what you picked.

Who guessed right?
Have that person pick something
for the next time.

Where are you?

Make believe you are
in this picture.
A tree is in front of you.
A bee is in back of you.
Where would you be standing?

Make believe you are someplace in this picture.
Tell a friend what things are around you.
Can your friend guess where you are?

Words to Know

front   lower   near
back   left   far
higher   right

Picture to Think About

Tell where the boy is by using the words in "Words to Know."

140

Questions to Answer

1. What are some things in front of you? In back of you?
2. What are some things on your left? On your right?
3. What are some things higher than your head? Lower than your head?
4. What are some things near you? Far from you?

Fun Things to Do

Have some friends close their eyes.
Hide something in the room.
Have your friends open their eyes.
Have them try to find what you hid.
Only answer questions like
"Is it near the door?" or
"Is it higher than the window?"
The person who finds what you hid
gets to hide it.

Some Science Words to Know

142

Unit 4   Light and Shadows

Unit 5   Time

Unit 6   Spaces and Places

(Acknowledgments continued from page 2)

De Wys, Inc./*M. Vanderwall,* 10 (bottom right). De Wys, Inc./*Victor Englebert,* 12(bottom). De Wys, Inc./*Leo De Wys,* 13 (right). De Wys, Inc./*Everett C. Johnson,* 61 (left). De Wys, Inc./*Whitney L. Lane,* 114 (right). De Wys, Inc./ *David W. Hamilton,* 122. Editorial Photocolor Archives/*Suntree,* 8 (bottom left). Editorial Photocolor Archives/*Peter Vadnai:* 44 (bottom), 115 (left). Editorial Photocolor Archives/*Paul Bernstein,* 60 (left). *Dwight Ellefsen,* 30 (bottom right). *John D. Firestone,* 124 (both). *Grant Heilman:* 31 (all), 36 (top and bottom right), 40. Grant Heilman/*Runk/Schoenberger:* 26 (bottom left), 54 (left). Grant Heilman/*George H. Harrison,* 135 (left). *Daniel D. Miller:* 77 (both), 78 (both), 79 (both), 81 (left), 82 (both), 85 (both), 86, 87 (both), 89, 91, 92 (all), 93, 98 (both), 101 (both), 102 (left), 103 (both), 105, 108 (top left), 109 (bottom). Monkmeyer Press Photo Service/*Bendick Associates,* 12 (top left). Monkmeyer Press Photo Service/*Freda Leinwand:* 18 (bottom right), 51 (bottom), 61 (bottom right). Monkmeyer Press Photo Service/*Mahon,* 27 (top left), 109 (top right). Monkmeyer Press Photo Service/*Hugh Rogers:* 29 (left), 50 (left), 58 (top). Monkmeyer Press Photo Service/*George Zimbel:* 43 (left), 74 (left), 102 (left). Monkmeyer Press Photo Service/*Mimi Forsyth:* 53, 108 (bottom right), 112 (top), 123 (left). Monkmeyer Press Photo Service/ *Dick Hufnagle,* 54 (bottom right). Photo Research Int.: 10 (bottom left), 11 (left), 18 (left and top right), 20, 33, 35 (both), 37 (top right), 39 (left), 44 (top left), 57 (right), 58 (bottom), 61 (top right), 66 (both), 67, 68, 69 (both), 75 (right), 90, 94, 99 (top), 100 (left), 110 (top), 113 (bottom), 117 (bottom), 118, 128, 131 (bottom), 132 (left), 140. Photo Research Int./*Everett C. Johnson,* 54, top right. Photo Research Int./*Bob Page,* 130 (bottom right). Root Resources/ *Earl L. Kubis,* 76 (left). Root Resources/*Delores Backe,* 135 (right). *Edward Simonek,* 42 (bottom). Tom Stack and Associates/*Tom Stack,* 26 (top right). Tom Stack and Associates/*James Belsanti,* 27 (bottom). Tom Stack and Associates/ *Warren Garst,* 38 (top right). Tom Stack and Associates/*Barbara Matt,* 76 (right). *Michael D. Sullivan,* 39 (top right). Michael D. Sullivan/*Dale Ahearn,* 13 (bottom). Sunrise Photos/*Rohn Engh:* 36 (left), 37 (top left), 109 (top left). Taurus Photos/*Marjorie Pickens,* 8 (top left). Taurus Photos/*Vance Henry,* 32 (top). Taurus Photos/*Bob McNerling,* 38 (top left). Taurus Photos/*Clarence Dickerson,* 74 (top right). *P. Treger:* 81 (right), 88 (left). *Larry P. Trone,* 70. *Paul Tucker:* 11 (right), 13 (top left), 16 (right), 28 (left), 30 (top right), 39 (bottom), 45 (top), 112 (bottom left), 114 (left), 115 (right), 134 (left). Van Cleve Photography/*Karen Phillips,* 12 (top right). Van Cleve Photography/ *William Means:* 27 (top right), 43 (right), 63, 83 (left), 110 (bottom), 111, 113 (top), 116, 129 (both). Van Cleve Photography/*Peter Fronk:* 37 (bottom), 45 (bottom). Van Cleve Photography/*Suzanne Seed,* 38 (bottom). Van Cleve Photography/*James Marchael,* 57 (left). Van Cleve Photography/*David Kelley,* 62. Van Cleve Photography/*Dave Logan,* 80 (right). Van Cleve Photography/ *Rohn Engh,* 99 (bottom). Van Cleve Photography/*Barbara Van Cleve:* 108 (top right and bottom left), 134 (right). Van Cleve Photography/*Audrey Ross,* 127. Van Cleve Photography/*Ron Larsen,* 130 (left). Zefa: 56 (left), 75 (left). Zefa/ *M. Wegler:* 10 (top), 51 (top right). Zefa/*Bert Leidmann,* 55 (bottom). Zefa/ *H. Lutticke,* 83 (top right). Zefa/*M. Pitner,* 88 (right). Zefa/*Dr. Lorenz,* 100 (right).